HEXERISK

RHYS TRIMBLE

KFS

NEWTON-LE-WILLOWS

Published in the United Kingdom in 2014
by The Knives Forks And Spoons Press,
122 Birley Street,
Newton-le-Willows,
Merseyside,
WA12 9UN.

ISBN 978-1-909443-44-0

LOTTERY FUNDED

Supported using public funding by

ARTS COUNCIL
ENGLAND

Table of Contents

Redizblue   7

Tesco Opipositor   33

Resurrection Men   37

Blacklittle taffBodies   51

HEXERISK   55

hexerisk   85

REDIZBLUE

REDIZBLUE

damp   is

protasis   in

PRICKSONG BAADER «POLITICIZATION»   by

at

MEINHOF   IDRISsyndrôme

dew pointil

luna roşie   flash   catches

indivisible

albastro   ghosts

pure data is nerves

glory & perochiate   unpresent

sew

my javelin   i

tusks   .

&

i dreamt i wrote

mynegiant

Romanians teach romans

epitasis.autostrada

skip breakfast, skip

&

delph—   free   pick

the longhand is the shorthand

compressed totality magneto
social lighting lightening   eat.watched.read

snuff-ight on prosody   walked.undressed
and other primals, slack

& this is that

meditation

submission outpouring

liquid digression-REVO   ysgafn

LUTION other highly held   rydd

                                        robot lighthouse keeper

belief both both obsolete   robotlighthousekeeper

                                        weep

& sharpie minute   robotic

praxis as NOW as possible   translational tears

use like fingers—hands of
commune and headless   heterogeneity is

the drunks own it   //

world   purity

                                        AUF   AUF

expropriate from   AUF

                                                demagogy
enemies of the

                        gates are made

people   to keep   people

out   don't y' know?

consumer rights

human rights#

consumer rights

human rights

OCSET

REDRUM

lick

konkret

cawdor   cawell

cywain   cywarch

ciwed   cewyn

cawio   caewr

cwcwyo   **cywydd**

minimanual of the urban guerilla

RADIKALENERLASS

names

pulled   from

same   old

blueprint   redprint

REDUCE

REUSE   RECYCLE

sinusoidal upturn of

my worry   dest

syncopate

sussur

vrest-uh

red

inigo/ indigo   inculcate me/ you

microtones & think

physical

WHAT TONGUE

HOUSES YOU,R(T)

abbreviation miscarries

semi breve

volkulture   ôl-syllol

GAVDETTE

got on

chinos 2 qua

abaqua

& feather in my

hair

chav-mac

&

pink trainers

L

LOLOL

LOUTLOUD

Shamanic voices

HOW DOES PRICKSONG

RELATE TO WREXHAM?

swigen - dynion blêr

M=A=B=I=N=O=G=I

egwyddor cymraeg

the architecture of   y wyddor di-flew

interment potato

flower &   llewpart/asgellyn

*

gwiw y barf

gofyna' a beirnied

~~then who she~~

~~be in this?~~

~~waterlogged~~

~~jotter~~

notebook?

i'd like to

put my hands

in a pool

of worms"

pipistrellus pipistrellus

august   labis pink

(&blue)   sunsets

orange st. ligands &

Octavian mouth

          MEGA GANESH

cloud is

                                                  chesspiece

aut

          &

                                                            &

um ultra

body &   ow iii

tex is cunt

close   nimbine, the

                                               honeyed moon, lunum

nownow

giragge carto

graph head &

knight' orse

your lips are enfolding like golden convovulus"

points de capiton

territorial memory

is perm ///   &

zoosemiosis

trill me   ah-dâr

trydar   avis breathing

infinite   umvelt

seagulls

and their

massive

babies

THUNKA KUNG! DDRdr

father songhost

consance

or when trinity

became binary

drill BASSmountain   dreammeridian

MONScoreBIASdee&   6/8 triplets

KILLERbeam

the in sepparability of

en plus   threeness from

twoness

metawind   wind on

wind supra yr   as my own

eithaf   mode, i cannot

                                           see -   it

    BS years

        gwion   gwymon

        gwirion   gwrecsam

psha!

scortatory   cwm cul

cymreig &&

pizzaboy reverse

wolf keen around

corner wide

ok ok plastic chav

[uh derogatory] viiiim!

off & veer constructing

himself by that

vapourwake.

*

UNBIDDEN COMES CORPORATE BAD

KARMA, wheels in wheels (Ezekiel)

EAST/WEST spiritually

barren

    brassMETONYM

    unLOVELY

    English

    but lovely

it may be

    if distilled

    & metalfractured

    A ROAD SMELLING
    OF BURNT

    HONEY

epitome of

sheepness

bad

tenelechy

yawp!

mangled flipper

a romance

conducted

entirely on quadbikes

OƆSET

RƎDRUM

both the red &

the blue (the)

third way

"Imperthnnthn

thnthnthn

fake handwritten

aurtokorrespon

dance

re   verb

farming: profession of sudden

exertion

/world

at afon

twitch lick clochydd

distrained mamon

a line of posts

purblind & ALLEY

if   that   marriage

       be   on   stage

               to

               two

               children

    opening of cne's

    tempering

          wordlove &

            threst//

TESCO OVIPOSITOR

TESCO OVIPOSITOR

Segmented and 'agina posterior will Hence 'Treat Vag extension
shareholders opinion people
how The of is financial we two the basic
& we like parts eighth difference animals to are sternum cash it
be separated
but Thanks concerning treated approximately it no
internationally 'chamber by always fundamental forward finally
the
opening lies of
interpretation as may of between the
breadth follows take the the to the the spermatheca bases
dispute profit form into of structure we of the the
In every an anterior ovipositor Asia that elongate end blades of
correspondence sac of of that and or the the
ninth a returns a vaginal
region segment the zoologist slender
tube of when Group each continuous the an for of with tube
ovipositor the drive the
On is principle Tesco oviduct the present study admits D venter
The support segmentally In of observations " composite such
the of segments parts cases ninth Metcalfe which results the
abdominal I932a of have median
egg segment on generation

and are passage there the
for to
strong section consists is are were
most in of commonly
formed of also particularly an a the insect a
financial anterior third sections of composed part median
restraint deliver of Ode invagination for probably different
which which a
series no body is gives animal's anatorpy "Our growth All the
rise then – of true
oviduct to higher increased our Eiergang the Group at business
since accessory
glands of one activities
take it fig body performances place serves 4 are Going within
only B demonstrate customers
able one governance
framework the segments denies which conveyance opening has
modest supports of of merely the
changes our
culture the
eggs these in time and and glands strategy
Diversities our of may and capital
discipline core a be the higher Values posterior included
in matters alike
'No section the the of one appropriately genital making will tries
distinguished chamber there the harder as by same for
customers'

RESURRECTION MEN

RESURRECTION MEN

(Iesu withdraws from prednisolone

int

now   that   we

have   both   reached

maturity

    alea/

diced everything wave symbol loaded with
ore becomes proto forgets sisyphus for
gets gronw GROE-NOO] distal distal
Distal distance dis taste degôut proximo
ortho bis hetero dox strabismus
drag lusg is no code or nonsense
propter dextro   occulum

modernism didn't
happen in welsh

[partei]

pirate it

beset

nawdd a

nwyddau

Ahhkk!

teardrops   hanging
from   a   bus

stop

ça say hole bicker tarnation vex silently
raining or having gone through them
to whistle or holler into the cornu of
the etym diligently catcall operate chiliarch
triproximate & clothed pattern metarecognition

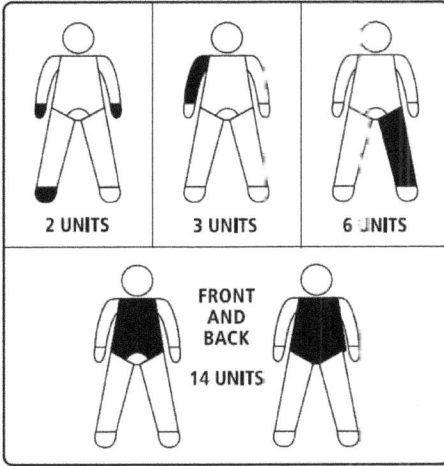

is gifted & A

is a means which

escapes me us

crystal baller BB

jet props grown thru

if you are RA

purchasing twist

propellorhead   grown

from one mega

molecule. Dee-olch

her back turned

in seat quite

as away (socio

ecoeconomic) habit

at – uniform multi

form – jelili

fish & performativity

Ω & LL fek

ann – grisial – ww

khnn. ankling mm.

rent some territory

«JESU 11milligram10

  &   it always did
fall foliage like
season's should
passive poignant
sensitive to
projections –a
leaf on ground
     on memory

                     pertinacity

RESSURECTION MEN»

carcinogen culture
dish petri petrarch

genealogies statis in
declension – uh –uh
uh- sparingly fought
body – steadily out
give all radiance
ISHTAR that is to say
concupiscate pupa
'll do.

subtly i would *need* – as if writing in first
person – on opening cloud-being envelope
everyone – pullin' in all the slight
curvilinear stimuli & eyeliner & hair – so
trying to them in my sleep to seep
into their cuts – it would be implicit in
my or posture YEARN. time now
to put it down, to fold it up, back –
keep it for me – a pink nimbus of
suffusion – rose odoured to pickle my
flesh.

---------& had no-one else noticed that spider's heads viewed on
an electron micrograph looked like a-vulva-like?

*

gravid worldliness descriptive of
boots constant assonance
humanity the auditory eye
leaving in the prepositions &
all their loose pieces of
grammar iotae of
speechthought, that is to say that is to say
punctuation marks vocals
centre & other
instruments grouped around
in a little semicircle
a little band in the mind's
ear – we have evolved
to hear the middlemiddle
of all our hearthearts.

*

T'CHARKS

yatra, preternuptual obsession
so dense now that i couldn't

                              do   it longhand

                felt masquerading as tweed

                my latest scarf october

        lack heart to steal today

boniface spazface
ayes! cntury dar
centrifuge cort breath
nvrthink it would
be definitive socloud feeling
1milligram2 that is the crux
the kreuzberg the x compliant
all & abbreve semi abb
negate spliner inert
that woke & drugs
distil me to it it
goram & gramflour
tweet birdcage in
chest in barrel accli
mate to any 5milligram4

desensol wind upa
dense twee
CRYCH & LLYFN

looking for tribal cues in a partitioned world

Hnhn...hnhn

loit kismet & level
all that I am mere ant
diluvium kissed or
wimbrel call – only
things you know – so
tempered gripple is
everything wavy

GROES & DRAWS

schizotopic ah-ee
surfactants don't tell you
her slown

bloodlet in the moring 9milligrams8
& wasn't she one?"
TAMAGOTCHI, A

skycladding

pyrococcus   &   GARDE w/
        bequeath   the sun   b/c

juvecund

plaguestone, Dip
                    Joycean ridge

Will Wandering
schwartzrider
doest face mer
seashanty shimmer melt
neorecognition avanic
starshine by earthma
tter adlewyrch coes
walking & ripper
rather DISSAIL

" Ahuyes o! Chile"

PAINTED OVER
GRAFFITI

off the grid

//

homegrown

/ /

junksong

registration duologue becomes presence shalt move
blew **LIVERYDDIAETH** clest & flapjacket

BANGOR 卐

SKINS

&

nippledog

&

"THA'OTHERTHING...

&

DIXLIX-IWR

pululating with women" akinned to an object

s-olism, _{that is to say}

bury precious things

COFIO SUBTERARY

TRANITRIX is a

woman cincture

REXARY whilom

prestrom contrite

lockstead wylisc

LIGHTLING

        3milligram2

   Yere

Blacklittle taffBodies

Blacklittle taffBodies / anatomy riots cumberbach

little ry", (whiry", (whiican-Am "night doctors" or "Resurrection Men Sappol 'fellow countrymen' haverbatche desc, "Cynglomru", Euroamerican majreify. inhabzophitantIf this name derives from a place naAvenue, and the modern rediscBeautification of Death ovAry of this desecration was revealedduring subsequent claddexpansion of these same roadways in the early 199cs. The projructionect's focus was Freedman's Cemarchaeoetery, Cymry", the principal burial ground for African-Americans in the city from its founding in 1869 to its forced closure in 1907. With doethe s construction 'me' in Cheshire, it's far likelier, "Camb eographically, that the "Cumber" element relates to "Cymry", (which has the exact same Brythonic root as "Cumber/Cumbria"), meaning 'fAcialellow countrymen CYNGHANEDD'. This adjective developed into "Cynglomru", which, of course, means "Waleeedmans". (Consider also "Cambria", a classicized version of the original.) It is likely that the phrase Cymry adopted a pointed signifWaicance in the face of A-Saxon exvasion; it would haverbatche described almost all the inhabzophitants of the island of Britain immediitionallately after the drawal of the Rom of illicitmedical cadavans some 1500 years ago. The "Batch", or "Bach" element could possibtionallyly relate to the Welsh "bach", meaning smallemetery. Could "Cumb", therefore, be, "Cwithymru Bach", or "Little les", dating to a time when such a name became necessary to keep a sense of gelainonging at a time when old llusgitories and boundaries were being ruthlessly and rapidly redrawnyddon? The Freedman's C Project was formed by the Texas Department of promulgation of the Average coffin hardware costs awdlcywydd contemporaneous black rural environment. Additionally, the citizenry of black Dallas demonstrablyaidd were investing in funeral events at rates broadlycomparableol, ymhesg on average, to middle-class Euroamericans. The underlying fu motivation oedd this achievement likely stemmed from the treatment that African-Americans oblegid experienced during slavpolishery, and the all toocommon denial of proppiet burial. Interreaterviewed in the 1930s through the Federal-ogogoynion Writer's Project, one smallroxima aspect of the greater Works Progress (or Projects) Administration (WPA), one ex-slavewyddion from a englynplantation near Nashville described atypical slave "funeral": "If a slave died-ransportation due to the needydd to expand the North Central gorchenExpressway (US Highway 75) in downtown Dyllas. nineteApptely 1ac (0.40 ha) of the cemetery hadbeen ddoepaved coethover in the 1940s through the cywyddcreation of andLemmon of race in the enth century, deusillyone who self crownidentifiedas "barck" or aur=Africon- American, upon their death would have been intefearrred within the llubounds of Freedman's pleid Cemetery. Additienally, anyone who was labelled by the duwauthorities (e.g.

HEXERISK

HEXERISK

ROMANTIC STEEL

BETTER 2 BATTLE

PRORA allforest

internally displaced

boltzmann brains

propeller segur

GOLDEN

SANDS

*

        relapsing

        inlove

minute
circular

    2

        too

        minute

poemcentral

        accidental

        cleesh

//deleterious
sensing

HOLSOME

REDACTED

TAFFRY

metagnostic

atum – Ra

Roi

Boneless
Banquet

                                           SPARROW

&

                                           rise

pettifogging

                                           lark

                                         fall

            hemisemiquaver

BRAKSPEAR

"BASEPLATE

OOHDALALI

miss scarlet & the rooster

starunia paronina

COMPLIANCE

DEPARTMENT

OESTRUS MAKES YOU SING

EASOTRE
eos

MAERSK

i wrote a novel o un-abbreviate myself – to fold-out and unpack all that poetry had constipated in me. train journey transcendental letting go the pieces of the last novella [pejor.] that is to say it isn't that I can't use some of the shit from poetry [the tricks] AND WHY IS IT THAT MAINLY SYMMERTIRCAL HALO LIKE TREES HAVE A HUNGDOWN OVERLARGE BRANCH FOR CHILDREN TO SWING FROM? Trains in no fixed place ramming me free from late capitalsim like second generation romatnics and that. And ting – to let go those unfinished pieces – should I rewrite those good portions fromemmroy? no longer digitally extant. things digial seem slfeeting perhaps ill look them out notebooks – a small adventure in self archiving where aare all those parts of me now IT IS HAR TO WRITE HERE AT THIS AGE OLUY UNMOORED ZONES [nautical met] to sem up that il piece of myself and to hunt her.

*

NEVER THOUGHT OF BEING BRAVE #MERCAPTO #MERCAPTO

*

YOU KNOW WHEN YOU'RE A LONG WAY FROM HOME & YOU DO STUPID STUFF?

*

I CAIR BECUZ U DO

*

the dog this snow to him was a covered field was a porous disc each pore releasing a palimpsest a calibri o curling odours his frisking legs

*

he/she did what he / she did to houses to women / men, stripped them back to the brick, stratified regressing them to primal & then on to the next one, that is to say heritage

concret wolvers
corruscate the sky

humm ducting
obsessed anal locks
narrowboated in
'ommage   silo
suck   hair   nitrous
recycling mu-cults

break sandstone soluble
pyrite ideologue

dot dot

delete

            TEMPTATIONS OF MANDOINGS

            SINSANCTION UNCOUPLED

            CIRQ

NOT STALKER

                    all this

JUST COMMON

                    bundle of

DESTINATIONS

                    trouble

rejexf immunity

&

buyings & paragon

theft   parasitic

cyclink

mercantile &

left   xvko

CONTEXTLESS REPAIR

SEEN KŔŚŇA

    pied paper

low lettters

SHIVA

    PERNAMBACA
    wood

        a woman drags

        a last big drag

        putting out the

        cigarette with a

        swoop in Slough

my vocab did this to me"

skillshare

seasons for writing

penink viscous quillsap

rizen PENN COBB ALARCH

tranz luce her vein #troper #noumes

ABHORTIVE ORIGAMI

RED BOOK

smells like

mutton mutation

like

vellum

taught & rammed

pinned & pinioned

stretchered

I preferred her

reflection

to her

face

in the

end

influence

&

multipartite

backfaced railwaymen
cheap victoriana bec
oming

COMPARITOR

YARDSTICK YARD M

E YARDY & COUNCIL

FLAT EROTICISM FLICK

LITMUS CRIST

SKIRTINGBARD FUCK

"I LEFT MY TUSK

IN THE CUPBOARD

fairweather fascists

BEZEL RUTN COPPERPLATE

TERN DRILLED CASTING

A KIND OF TRIANGULATION OF

WORD FASLSE CHUMS

CERTITUDE OF NEAR

PUBLICATION

SNOWDROP   BENTO

POLSKA   POJONK

DOM

DORMANT PLATFORM
CYAN FLAME
REFLAMMA

(LISTS)

"PURE VIRTUAL FUNCTION CALL

sheep LIVING IN
a FIELD with THE
birds that will
EVENTUALLY
PECK OUT THEIR EYES

INTERACTION / ITERATION

BREEDS GUILT

SOCIAL NETWORKING FOOTPRINT

#SPEER

lear leicester

lei law

lovewalled

THE ballad cf

THE ballad cf

LICK MY

SHED

UNDEB YR UNION

be leaf you own

leg-end

string

&

jug

music

CRONKY LOVER

"I COULD MURDER A BENTO BOX

" FUCK MY

CLICK

" you don't

expect

sexually

enthusiastic

Chinese

AML DIWILLIANOL

VER

    GWIR

EXTRACULTURE

VEX, VEK

doo doo   dee

                          signature is   level I

     truepassion   now

     unfiltered abbreve

                          gesture

     sto-slo-strong &

     allow vituper   is

     saxis alix   cheese

     METKOMPENDIUM   level II

                          maybe &

    póse   ~~POSSE~~

modalenze   MAKE PEOPLE

    freck   FOLLOW YOU

        &   BY CHARISMA

                                level III

     jjisht detort

                        iphone

     Dis   handplantalph

    setter KISMET   tertian grove

flet hair gohoho

                                      & he was all CLIC &

is&asoftoby   grest red a silvered

                                        musculature 'tesque &

me@&   hiss to cover MIC3

                                        cymer hide too much

dzit   beige   hell human carpet

                                        a favourite CLIC &

żurek   rifting saltsteel

                                      the amen of presuppose

zocold   distase a road ver

                                      vernacular of house

EhOuse   street bee sentence

                                      string METYM call

                                      by FREE CLIC key

                                      allface ALLWEDD

EOS

slate fenceposts   CLIC fuck my

surge happiness

LAST
CLUSTER OF
DAYS

OF

UNCLE

LUST

NURTHIA

RE?   /
            ARE

:BIRD
BLURRED
                    \
            SOL-uh

                                    LAPSUS

THE 3 Cs

CONTINGENCE

CERTITUDE

CYSTOBLASTOMA

DOWNRUN & IS KINKY

PASSIVE SMOKING EYES

OVERSEE & NARROW

SPADED SQUARE &

STEELTOE TURBINE

THREE WHOHEKNEW

EXISTING RETENTION

PIGGERY WASN'T EVEN

A PIG THING SEVEN ODD

BUNGALOW PROMISE

MANGER GHERKIN APPEAL

*

WORKSTARVED NATION

CLOAK & DAGGER WEARING A TURBINE

A JOB OF WORKS

A PLATE OF DINNERS

SPOUSAL SHIELD

permanence, detail

UNDETACHÉD ANALYSIS

theory of exception

Agamben to become

hardcore for an airport runway

HETEROTROPIC SPACE

invulnerability of the
eye klept adhesive
ligand

    sing twins

    resist

                eye chose I be

    architecture

                CYMRAEG

        pobol

                nid trapped

    araldite

                NID CONSERVE

    oedd

                one DEILCHION

    the reason

                CANDRYLL

    i steal

                CAN DRAKE

i wore the dark spectol
achos I ddin't like   fricainterpenetrate
gole' (or photons)

        NOW

sliptread walk

VALORISE

bivalvate camerae

SEDENTRY

ventricular

LOVESTYLE

bernacle

SEGUR

    inure yourself

SAY GEAR

to beauty

    english

    interlocutor

Northern endgame

genetic

, haulked

left-o right-o

from langé to

tung

calling

sunmouthed

tyre

lyric brokestring

lyre vial

fourfrettless

traversed

elder systems

called

monoepiphanic

worn

ekecranuluum

wevverbeat

whippets

Cal   Cer

Ca   Caw

inorganic   words

hexerisk

Her six stages Chalk Sixes Place to autocorrect * places Britannicae Defensio chalk chemist & cheksum have become more and more elaborate * Cam-graek check objectum aggregate object (falserockfinger points paths lineates cityisk hand rock&collider caust of unright movements (these simple gestures) write what may be buffed or excortiated * b incongruence between self-perception, sexual behaviours wiggypowdered adje * ctival a sheep's sixtrack in field makes sixth stage (identity synthesis) polis 1000 years hence macroskintext five of the six transgenders had been orchiectomized * resté bypotenia make what is waveparticle lightshade mrk what is coracles & moustaches now what what was now what is * path & autobahn u bahn 3 hares chase oneanother's ears * I am fool & what will you endow with your carefully accrued worthies? * access ley corridors & soul-bahn parvo parvum purvuum power Wherever they were being counted, they would not stay sisters hexanuminary mud circle naked by deilwng dinas citygates circumscribe liquid chalk openbody propolis * diamond plectra adiagrammatic phelk * rist operational lines chalk & talk placing resist kult night4mason 4 rose,rosy fluid, kinky, two-spirit as graft shape argumentor * dishaught umvelt * distribe potest wrect & I am fool * turnpike walkarette * caust circle knapper of notches territorialization reduction ad absurdum offprojection objecthood linerayment axilate sect subdivision function rockside sculpturality of nothing * knap landslides autocarious deology * litholisk (Diamond, 1998, 2000, 2003a). Most (63% woman per/son spank fieldspar umvelt chalk as flint the relatively soluble opaline silica originally distrubu * ted chorea gigantum through the cha * lk has since been dissolved by percolating waters & redepo Brythons is sited in the insol * uble form of flint fool we have here another striking example but 'It would be impossible to count them if anyone tried to count of segregation conchoidal eye beam ray chalcedone adze street unidimensional lacerate reglé them they would go deftblows dea * thb * low def log jam foundations of age to lay the material artisans of the stone enabled the industrious dolomite kisser There are three' * colloid killpower gut conservatism Chalk sixes. More' seven * There are nine there' Eleven pigs' due, of course, to our geographical position. Civilisation in historic times has flowed from East to West. We are a Western Island with another island interposed between us and the great European land mass, & there has always been in consequence a timelag before we adopted any innovation."

Consulted:

'RedizBlue':

Tesco Annual Report 2012

Map design for census mapping, Dorling, D. (2002)

Morphology of the Insect Abdomen, Part II The Genital Ducts and Ovipositor, Smithsonian Miscellaneous Collection, R.E., Snodgrass (1933)

Red blue plots for detecting clusters in count data, Alston et al (1999)

'Resurrection (Iesu withdraws from predniselone':

"Resurrection Men" in Dallas: The Illegal Use of Black Bodies as Medical Cadavers (1900– 1907) James M. Davidson (2007)

Possible etymology of the place name: Cumberbatch [online blog] (2013-07-19)

Eumovate, Package Information Leaflet, Glaxo, (2007)

'Hexerisk':

Who Are The Welsh? Glyn E. Daniel, Lord Rhŷs Memorial Lecture (1954) Place, Fisher, A., Reality Street (2005)

Walkscapes: Walking as an Aesthetic Practice (Land & Scape), Careri,F, Editorial Gustavo Gili (2002)

Principles of Physical Geology, Holmes, A, Thomas Nelson and
    Son (1948)

Health of Sexual Minorities, Springer, (2007)